IZZARD INK PUBLISHING COMPANY
PO Box 522251
Salt Lake City, Utah 84152
www.izzardink.com

Library of Congress Cataloging-in-Publication Data

Names: Hartman, Robert S., 1910-1973, author. | Hurst, Clifford G.
(Clifford Guin), 1953- editor. | Blakemore, Catherine, editor.
Title: Wit & wisdom : inspiration for living fully / quotes by Robert S.
Hartman ; edited by Clifford G. Hurst and Catherine Blakemore.
Other titles: Quotations. Selections | Wit and wisdom
Description: Salt Lake City : Izzard Ink Publishing, 2021.
Identifiers: LCCN 2020051681 | ISBN 9781642280418 (paperback)
Subjects: LCSH: Hartman, Robert S., 1910-1973--Quotations. |
Values--Quotations, maxims, etc. | Conduct of life--Quotations,
maxims, etc. | Wit and humor--Quotations, maxims, etc.
Classification: LCC BD232 .H332 2021 | DDC 121/.8--dc23
LC record available at https://lccn.loc.gov/2020051681

Cover & Book Design by Treadaway Co.
First Edition January, 2021

Paperback ISBN 978-1-64228-041-8

WIT &
WISDOM

WIT &
WISDOM

Inspiration for Living Fully

QUOTES BY ROBERT S. HA

Edited by Clifford G. Hurst and Catherine F

TABLE OF CONTENTS

PREFACE

Wit, it can be said, is the compact expression of wisdom.

Robert S. Hartman wrote with both wit and wisdom. Many times, though, his wit gets buried in demanding and lengthy prose.

In this book, we have extracted the wit from the wisdom of a selection of Hartman's writing so that more of the world can learn from this man's genius. It's a quote book. It consists entirely of Hartman's own words. But, in small doses.

We have pulled vital ideas, thoughtful considerations, and clever remarks from seven of Hartman's published pieces plus one heretofore unpublished manuscript that are soon to be published by the Hartman Institute. We present these quotes in an order that, we believe, best tells the story of formal axiology, from general principles to practical application.

If you want to grasp the essence of formal axiology in this way, then read it from front-to-back. If you are merely curious, turn to any page at random and you're sure to stumble upon something that will excite, challenge, or inspire you.

If your curiosity is whetted, then we invite you to go to the original source. For every quote we identify the source from which it was taken.

The 2nd Edition of Webster's Unabridged Dictionary gives us many definitions of "wit," all of which speak of Robert Hartman.

A "wit" originally referred to a person of extraordinary intellectual powers or constructive genius. **That was Hartman.**

To have "wit" means to have mental sharpness and alertness, intellectual quickness and penetration, acumen. "It includes," continues Webster, "having a readiness in seizing upon and expressing brilliantly and amusingly ideas which are startlingly incongruous in association." **That, too, was Hartman.**

Who else could have said, "Your inner Self, your humble Being, is what makes dogs lick you. That's all." **Hartman, of course.**

Wit, continues Webster, may also express itself in the form of "deft and spontaneous play with unperceived analogies, often with a critical or satirical application." In describing how we can end wars, Hartman writes satirically: "When nations give wars, we should not attend." **Vintage Hartman.**

There are more than 130 such gems from the pen of Robert Hartman on the following pages. Read. Ponder. Then share this book with others. Together, let's inspire the world with the wisdom of Robert S. Hartman by sharing his wit.

EDITORS

Clifford G. Hurst, Ph.D
& Catherine Blakemore   2020

The following quotes are organized topicly rather than by source material. We've included with each quote an abbreviated reference title (shown below) to correspond with the list of Hartman's published works at the end of this book. We encourage you to explore Hartman's thought through these quotes and his legacy through these additional works.

Moral Quandary

Humanity today faces a moral quandary. Collectively, we know how to harness technology to improve our physical well-being. But when it comes to morals, we lag behind. We remain morally at the same stage as we were technologically in the Middle Ages. Then we had astrology; now we have astronomy. Then we had alchemy; now we have chemistry. Then we had blood-letting with leeches; now we have the marvels of modern medicine. Yet morally speaking, humankind is no better off than we were 400 years ago. We still have wars, hate, violence, discrimination, and degradation of others. Why? In this chapter, Hartman describes the quandary we are in.

"Just as the natural philosophers developed mathematics as a tool for understanding nature, so moral philosophers have been trying to develop a tool for understanding moral nature. This tool is called Axiology or value theory."

"Our social and moral knowledge,
thus, is in the alchemistic stage,
and our social and moral life bears
witness to it."

"There is no objective, universal philosophical system which helps us understand any text of ethics or of philosophy in general. But there is a universal system in natural science by means of which one can understand any scientific text whatsoever: mathematics."

"What we need is a science of ethics. Just as the natural sciences have developed from the vagueness of commonplace conjecture to precise disciplines, so ethics must develop from commonplace conjecture to scientific precision."

"We are living in two ages. With our emotions we are still in the Stone Age, hating and loving, envying and desiring as primitively as the cave man; with our intellect we are projecting planetary travel."

"What we need is very simple. We need a new Spirit. We need a new Science. We need a new Method."

"We shall either die or live abundantly. There is no middle course. And it must be our generation that shall not pass before these things are done."

REVOLUTION

"The evil of our time, as that of all times, is due not so much to the evil in our hearts as it is to the ignorance of our minds."

"We are scientific masters but moral morons."

"*The difference is again similar to that between alchemy and chemistry. Alchemy was an unconnected multitude of hit and miss stabs at nature; most present-day ethics is an unconnected multitude of hit and miss stabs at moral nature.*"

"Natural philosophy has changed the face of the earth to such an extent that neither Julius Caesar nor Columbus would recognize it. Unfortunately, Jesus Christ would recognize it only too well. For the inner world in which he was interested and where he hoped to establish the Kingdom of God, looks as barren and sterile, as chaotic and anarchic, as neglected and uncultivated as in his day."

"What we are fighting against are institutions gone mad."

"What follows, then, is an attempt to de-mystify and sensitize, to make the vague, the intuitive, and the chaotic in the world of human values intellectually clear, to show how formal axiology can lead to awareness of the several worlds we live in, to suggest a meaningful score for what could be a harmony of life."

On Philosophy

Part of the reason we are in a moral quandary is due to the habitual practice of philosophy. In a sense, we are mostly all Aristotelians. We seek to understand moral nature by studying those things about human nature that we can observe with our senses, then we categorize our understanding in words. Interminably thereafter, we debate the meaning of those words. Before Galileo, natural scientists did the same thing. Today, however, natural scientists have moved on to explore the structure that underlies the physical world's observable aspects — its mathematical properties. What philosophers and social scientists must do is seek to understand the structure that underlies the moral world.

"The new moral science ought to revolutionize our moral understanding itself and hence our moral practice, in the same way that natural science has revolutionized our understanding of nature and our sensitivity to it ... It ought to teach us more profoundly the art of living."

"What mathematics is to natural philosophy, formal axiology is to moral philosophy."

"*This science of values must be as definite as is the science of mathematics, and it must be to the social sciences as mathematics is to the natural sciences.*"

"The tension between moral ignorance and scientific knowledge cannot be relieved by scrapping knowledge. The only alternative is to apply the methods of scientific research to the nature of man. Our educated intellects must be joined by educated emotions to form moral intelligence."

"If we truly want to know what value is, we must know scientifically and must stop knowing philosophically."

KNOWLEDGE

"He [Galileo] invented an entirely new frame of reference in which to think of heaven and earth. His simple formulae opened up — by reason, not by magical persuasion — the storehouse of nature from which we have drawn the energy of the modern age."

KNOWLEDGE

"For the first time, I feel, scientific knowledge and mastery of physical nature can be matched by scientific knowledge and mastery of our moral nature. Natural science has changed the world; value science, too, once it is known, developed, and applied, is bound to change the world."

On Goodness

In order to be good, we need to figure out what it means to know the good. This is harder than it seems. Philosophers have argued for centuries about the very meaning of "good." Hartman devoted his life to answering the question, "What is good?" Understanding goodness and choosing to live a good life are achievements; they don't happen automatically. Evil is automatic. Good must be earned.

"If the world were not primarily good and orderly, most planes would crash, most cars collide, most people be sick — and insurance companies broke. That they are flourishing is a proof that evil and contingency are a statistically small element in the orderly universe. Hence faith is rationally justified.
We should have the courage to have faith, faith in faith."

"Between the good of tomorrow and the evil of today stands the ignorance of man about himself."

"In Hitler at school I saw evil
organizing itself and I made it my
life's work to organize good. This
made it necessary for me to know
the nature of good and evil."

REVOLUTION

"What happened to the Germans can happen to any nation. It is likely to happen if technological societies do not muster their moral energies. As it is, our moral and social life lacks intelligent organization."

"*Our greatest affliction at the present time is not so much ill will as ignorance of the good.*"

REVOLUTION

"*The good, we seem to feel, takes care of itself. Actually, the good is our achievement. The evil takes care of itself.*"

"The greatest power on earth is the good will and decency in the heart of each human being."

On Values

"Value" is a word frequently bantered about. But few people
have successfully explored exactly what is meant by value,
not to mention its underlying logic. Here, Hartman states
emphatically that modernist intellectual assertions that
facts are objective and values are subjective, is wrong. We
simply need a way to study values in the social world as
objectively as scientists today study facts in the physical
world.

"*The frequently made distinction between fact and value as the realm of objectivity and subjectivity, respectively, is invalid.*"

"*The borderline between fact and value is extremely thin yet runs extremely deep in an invisible crack in our understanding.*"

"*If there is very little literature about the value of logic, there is almost none about the logic of value.*"

"Value has not been made an object of orderly thinking. It has not been made really the subject of a theory; and 'value theory' is a euphemism."

KNOWLEDGE

*"Values permeate the whole
of human existence and are
presupposed wherever there is
thought and action based upon
thought. The mission of philosophy
is to make the unconscious
recognition of values conscious and
by doing so to give value-judgments
a coherent structure."*

KNOWLEDGE

"The difference between natural
science and value science is that the
former applies to events, while the
latter applies to the meanings of
events. Value, we may say,
is meaning."

Axioms and Axiology

Axiology is the study of values. To Hartman, for the study of values to be something more than the mere subjective categorization of words related to value, the subject must be approached scientifically. A science of value must be derived, he maintains, from a small number of axioms. An axiom is often a starting point in logic.

The theory of formal axiology that Hartman developed is an axiomatic theory. At times, Hartman wrote that formal axiology is based upon one axiom; at other times, he alluded to there being a few axioms. These axioms give us a way to understand the structure of values and human nature in the same way that the mathematical structure underlying the physical world gives scientists a tool for understanding physical nature.

Hartman's underlying axiom of formal axiology is that "goodness is concept fulfillment." From that underlying axiom, he deduces three levels of value, the Intrinsic (I), the Extrinsic (E), and the Systemic (S).

"The axiom
of axiology
shows that
moral value
has primacy
over economic
value."

FORMS

"All things of human experience,
that is, all things in space and
time—all things that are not
scientific constructs—must be
valued axiologically."

FORMS

"Scientific axiology, based on purely formal equations, thus arrives at truly revolutionary results. It ought to be destined, and I believe it is, to bring forth a new moral world. For the real revolutions are not those fought in the streets but are those of the spirit."

"*If I say that a thing is good and you say that it is bad, we do not invalidate axiology, we only apply it differently; in reality, we confirm it by our difference.*"

The trouble with axiology is that we do not yet have a system within which value judgments find their place, as mathematical judgments do in mathematics .... Thus values have the usual epistemological status of things unknown, no more nor less than, say, flying saucers.

"It is my conviction that through formal axiology the deep, eternal values of life can be made intellectually articulate."

Developing the "I"

The intrinsic nature of humans is illustrated with examples in this chapter. Intrinsic value and valuation comprise what Hartman refers to as the "I" dimension of his theory of formal axiology. The intrinsic dimension is hard to explain but can be intuitively grasped. The quotes by Hartman in this chapter give a sense of the importance and the scope of the intrinsic dimension of value and valuation in human development.

"It is an easy logic if we will do just one thing: set the human person into the center of every situation."

FORMS

"The kind of knowledge relevant to intrinsic valuation is exceedingly rare .... It is the kind of knowledge possessed in the highest degree of the creative genius .... This kind of knowledge is direct, immediate, 'intuitional'; it is that of the complete person encompassing the world. It is not a matter of intellect but of character."

"This science of human values must be based on the supremacy of the human individual and the human conscience."

REVOLUTION

"A good man, according to many
teachers of ethics, is one who
develops all his potentialities
to the full."

"The most important singular thing that each one of us possesses is himself. Each of us is given to himself and our task in life consists in knowing ourselves more and more, in familiarizing ourselves with ourselves more deeply, in becoming increasingly more who we are."

"I am moral in the degree that I am who I am, not in the degree that I do what I am doing."

"While physical nature has yielded to man's inquiring mind and is opening up to him ever richer treasures, man's inner nature is a wasteland he has never bothered to explore with equal determination."

"*You must have the feeling that you are here for a reason. If you have that feeling, you have intrinsic depth; if you don't have it, well, then, you have to develop it.*"

"It is not what you do that counts,

but the spirit in which you do it.

You have it within you to fill a

particular place in the world. If you

move toward that place, large or

small, great or not-so-great, then

you have the feeling of meaning,

of transparency."

"Any 'aha' experience is a minute mystic experience."

"*Physically you're only a little person on a huge globe, but within you, you can, if you fulfill your Self, contain the whole world, all humanity, indeed the vastness of the universe and God.*"

"I am morally good if I am as I am. All the words of ethics mean this very same thing, this identification of myself with myself; being sincere, honest, genuine, true, having self-respect, integrity, authenticity."

"If you are alive to the spirit, your knowledge of the world will grow of itself, as you need it."

"Sometimes, unfortunately, our intellect blocks our attempt to become alive to the spirit within us — to become Self-aware."

"To the degree that I am I, I am a morally good person. Moral goodness is the depth of man's being himself."

"To be is probably the most difficult and, at the same time, the most important task of our moral lives."

"Your inner
Self, your
humble Being,
is what makes
dogs lick you.
That's all."

Developing the "E"

The extrinsic realm of value feels more comfortable to many of us than do the other two dimensions. Hartman reports that most of us live primarily in this realm. It's important that we understand and honor our extrinsic value, but it's equally important that we keep this dimension in context. Our extrinsic self is best considered in balance with the "S" and "I" dimensions, especially the "I."

FORMS

"The knowledge relevant to extrinsic valuation is the knowledge of the world of things, of the order and classification of things which correspond to their actual variety. This is the valuation of common sense, of sound situational understanding. Here we have the capacity of comparison, of judging the present in terms of the future, that is, of anticipation, and the solid open-mindedness that used to distinguish the American mind."

"We are experts only at social living — and that is only one world among three. Thus we really live very limited lives."

"Ninety-five percent of the people
in the developed countries, East and
West, capitalist and communist,
live mostly in the world of extrinsic
value. The vast majority of them
believe this is the only really
important world there is,
neglecting their inner Self."

"To scramble around on the
treadmill of extrinsic value is not
only immature, it is inefficient, for
it shuts up your infinite powers and
lets them lie idle. It prevents you
from really living."

"Now if you are not aware of your Self, you live only a little, and this is an ever-present danger in a socially well-organized society. It's so easy just to coast along."

"Extrinsically, a thing has more properties — and more value — than systemically, but its value still is bounded."

"Everyone gets classified and is valued as an insurance agent, mechanic, teacher, housewife, mother, pupil, or what have you. This we call the social value or extrinsic value. Money, for example, usually has only extrinsic value. But all social or extrinsic values are limited."

"Most of us are not our Selves. We play roles."

DEVELOPING THE "S"

Developing the "S"

The systemic realm is conceptually the simplest of the three realms of value. As Hartman writes, it is the realm of "yes/no" of "on/off" — a dimension of value that permits no shades of distinction. While it is important that we develop the systemic dimension, when it comes to human relations, it is even more important that we keep it in its place, as subordinate to the extrinsic and intrinsic realms.

FORMS

"Systemic truth is consistency. That is true which fits the system. Facts as they actually are ... are of no relevance for systemic truth; for it is not facts that fit into the system but schemata of facts, and sometimes even schemata produced by the imagination. The mind does not have to go outside itself and its processes to determine systemic truth."

FORMS

"Not all systemic valuation is evil. It
is evil only when it is a transposition
— when applied to situations where it
is inappropriate. Many things in our
individual and social life must be valued
systemically. Scientific constructs must
be valued in this way, and the rigorous
discipline of systemic valuation in
general is necessary for modern society
and is precisely what ... American
education is lacking, as against
European education."

FORMS

"The subjects of logical or systemic valuation are things in a minimum relationship: as elements of a system or as schemata. A schema is less real than any empirical thing. When human beings are valued systemically they are less real than, say, a piece of paper. In a bureaucratic procedure a person does not exist unless he has a birth certificate."

"*The world of systemic value is the haven of those who lack Self, that is, fully differentiated intrinsic value, and it is hell for those who are alive consciously to their own inner Self.*"

FORMS

"Knowledge of systems is purely intellectual and abstract .... The pure specialist as such only knows systems; as a specialist he looks at the world itself as a system. In doing so, the world becomes distorted ... Specialization thus becomes a curse of the modern world ... Thus, our very (scientifically) specialized civilization brings us continuously into the danger of systemic valuation."

"Systemic value is the value of conformity to a system... This kind of valuation only knows two values, perfection or non-existence, it sees everything as dichotomy, as either white or black."

"Oddly enough, my own philosophy has taught me the relative unimportance of my own philosophy."

"Systemic value is morally
neutral, like the law, like science.
We can't live without system, but
we can overdo it."

"Systemic value must be overcome by extrinsic and intrinsic values."

Integration of I, E, S

Many value theorists argue whether value resides in the object being valued or whether it is inherently a function of the person doing the valuing. To Hartman, it resides in both. In formal axiology, the value dimensions of I, E, and S can refer both to value objects and to ways of valuing them. Thus, Hartman distinguishes between value and valuation. It is the astute combination of human valuations of value objects that gives rise to the richness of formal axiology. It is learning how to effectively integrate our understanding of all three levels of value with their appropriate levels of valuation that poses both the challenge and the opportunity to live life axiologically.

FORMS

"The categories of axiology can be applied to anything. Anything whatever, from the lowest to the highest, can be valued in all three processes, systemically, extrinsically, and intrinsically."

"Systemic language is technical and precise; extrinsic language is empirical and descriptive; intrinsic language is metaphorical."

FORMS

"The whole development of our time thus conspires to bring about systemic valuation. Against this, the men of common sense — who value extrinsically — and those of spiritual insight — who value intrinsically must stand together. Their means of fighting must be the articulation of sanity: the rational understanding of valuation."

"All technical achievements are worth nothing if not coupled to achievements of the soul."

"Power comes to him who believes
in the good, and that the good is the
balance between mind and soul,
body and spirit."

"*Any government is a system dominated, to a large extent, by systemic values. The art of governing consists in adjusting as much as possible the systemic values — of bureaucracy, red tape and so on — to human values.*"

"We must let it be known that we
have the opportunity to live in three
worlds, the systemic world of rules,
the social world of the senses, and
the moral or spiritual world of our
inner Selves — and therein to live
balanced, meaningful lives."

The Hartman Value Profile

Once we recognize that each of the three levels of value can be valued in each of the same three ways of valuation, we have a basic understanding of how the theory of formal axiology gave rise to the development of the Hartman Value Profile or HVP for short. All we need to add to our understanding is that each value dimension can be valued in ways that enrich its properties or in ways that diminish its properties. Recognition of that leads to the 18 words or phrases that are used in the HVP. To this, we add the idea that the instrument can measure one's value capacities as they relate to the outside world and as they relate to the self, thus the two-part nature of the assessment. In this chapter, Hartman outlines some of the many potential applications of the Hartman Value Profile.

"The Hartman Value Profile
(HVP) is a strictly axiological
test which measures the person's
capacity to value."

"The HVP measures the deviation of the subject's own score from a theoretical score based on formal axiology. This logic determines the correctness or incorrectness of value judgments. The test therefore measures the capacity for making value judgments."

"*The test consists of two parts,
the first measuring the capacity
to value the world, the second
measuring the capacity to value
one's own self.*"

"A distinction must be made between value
in general and specific values (interests,
preference, etc.). The capacity to value
in general is to specific value interests or
preferences as the capacity to see color is to
specific color interests or preferences. Before
testing a person as to his preference for, say,
green or red, he ought first to be tested as to his
capacity for seeing color. A color-blind person,
obviously, cannot have a valid judgment as
to his preferences for red or green. Similarly,
before testing a person as to his preference for,
say, religious, theoretical, economic, or political
values, it would be good first to test him as
to his capacity to value in general. Since his
interests are specific values, his capacity to
distinguish them depends on his capacity
to value in general."

"There are both perceptual and conceptual sources of value errors: one can see the thing wrongly; one can believe it has another name from what it has; one can misunderstand its concept; one can wrongly apply the concept to the thing, etc. A test of axiological valuation must take into consideration all these possibilities of value error."

"Systemic valuation is the model of dogmatism and prejudice, of rigid and schematic thinking, and of formal construction."

"What is valued in extrinsic valuation is not the thing itself but its possession of the intensional properties of its concept, or the class it belongs to. Fulfillment by a thing of an abstract concept constitutes extrinsic value."

"Intrinsic valuation is the model of creativity, spontaneity and commitment, of emphatic and empathic thinking. This kind of thinking has been called, in psychology, Being Cognition."

"Systemic value, extrinsic value,
and intrinsic value are the value
dimensions. They constitute a
hierarchy of richness, with intrinsic
value richer in qualities than
extrinsic value, and extrinsic
value richer in qualities than
systemic value."

"Systemic value (S), extrinsic value (E), and intrinsic value (I) can themselves be valued in terms of each other. These valuations of the value dimensions in terms of each other give rise to the calculus of value."

"There are, for each test, 6.4 quadrillion possible answers."

"The test is extremely sensitive and shows up very subtle deviations from the norm. These deviations have their basis in the person's own value pattern. The pattern expresses itself in specific values, interests or preferences, but the test does not measure the latter; it measures the underlying value pattern."

"To young people, the test shows up not only their general capacity but also their valuational strengths and weaknesses, as well as the value dimensions in which they are particularly gifted. The test thus may serve as complement to interest and aptitude tests."

"In the case of executives, the results of the test may serve to channel activities both of themselves and their associates in the direction of their particular valuational strength, and thus to increase their decision-making capacities. It may serve to check activities incompatible with the test results."

"In the case of groups, the test
shows up the compatibility and
incompatibility of the individuals
in it and provides a number
of classifications comparing
individuals in their various
functions within the group."

"In the case of matching people,
as mates, partners, associates,
collaborators, and in all cases of
teamwork, the test will indicate
compatible and incompatible
value patterns."

"In the case of mental health
prevention, the test discovers
potential suicides and other
emotional and intellectual disorders
before actual symptoms appear."

"In the case of psychotherapy, psychoanalysis, etc., the test, when given at the first session with the patient, indicates the strengths and weaknesses of the person and thus gives an initial guide for the direction of treatment. Given periodically, it pinpoints the results of the treatment."

"*The healthy person who does not require psychotherapy or psychoanalysis yet desires a new meaning of his life, can be helped by the test to revise and reorder his values. This process is called Axiotherapy. Axiotherapy is similar to other value-directed therapies, such as Logotherapy.*"

On Economics

The development of the Hartman Value Profile is one important consequence of Hartman's development of his value theory, but it is not the only one. Hartman wrote prolifically about other social matters and used the lens of formal axiology for his critique and recommendations. He was greatly excited about what he referred to as a third wave of capitalism to come. It is to be a form of capitalism that evokes a partnership between capital and labor. It is to be built upon cooperation, not competition. It will make capitalists out of workers by allowing them to share in the profits of their labor.

"If human cooperation is mobilized, it is the most powerful economic resource at our disposal."

FORMS

"The revolution that will abolish
poverty is not a political but a
moral revolution. From the axiom
of axiology follows the theorem that
the degree of poverty in a society is
the measure of its lack of moral and
social responsibility; the wealth of a
nation is a direct function of
social morality."

"If formal axiology is correct then we should be able to observe that, in practice, economic systems function better when they are more moral and worse when they are less so."

REVOLUTION

"The wrong man in the wrong place seems to be a more 'normal' phenomenon than the right man in the right place. The majority of social maladjustments could be avoided if there existed a scientific system assisting everyone in his own development, in the knowledge of his own potentialities, and in finding his place in society."

"This means that the method of production must be adjusted to the nature of man, rather than man to the nature of production. Thus human relations become an intrinsic part of industry, and ethics enters as a creative element into the economic process."

"*Alongside this new ethic develops a new logic. The logic of the class struggle was a logic of subtraction. It saw in the success of one the failure of the other, in the prosperity of one the poverty of the other .... The new logic is that of addition. It sees the success of one in the success of the other, the prosperity of one in the prosperity of the other.*"

"The worker appears as a person, interested in the success of the whole company and participating in it; the employment relationship is lifted to a higher level. In this way a new capitalism appears on the scene, making capitalists out of workers and transforming the capitalism of the few into the capitalism of the many."

"*The new employment relation is a team relation, a partnership, not only in production and profit sharing, but also in human community. The worker is no mere fabricator of goods, but a person, and the employment relation becomes one of trust, and even, as we shall see, of friendship.*"

"The 'company' becomes a moral community."

"The two obsolete systems, the capitalist and the socialist, are built on antithesis: the class struggle. The new system is their synthesis and reconciliation."

"Only when the worker actually owns himself and his work and participates in the fruit of his labor and the prosperity of his factory do we have a new system."

"The practice of profit sharing
in partnership ... starts from the
premise that the worker has a right
to that part of the profit which he
has himself created."

"This science (of moral economy) has not yet been written nor has it even been conceived. It arises out of the practice of the new system of partnership. In this sense the present book can be regarded as a treatise in moral economy."

On War and Peace

Hartman wrote that his life was "marked" by war. He was a young child in Germany when his father went off to fight in WWI. He escaped Germany, and then Sweden, in the face of Nazi aggression. For the remainder of his life, Hartman pondered deeply about the causes of war and the prospects for peace. His theory of formal axiology gave him a lens through which to evaluate humankind's propensity for war. War and peace, Hartman concluded, are matters of morality; they are matters of the human heart. What is needed, he concluded, is a concerted effort to understand peace... a national agenda for peace research.

REVOLUTION

"*The economic and political problems with which we are so much concerned are trivial as compared with the problems of the human soul with which we are so little concerned. War and peace, I now know, are not problems of politics or economics or geography or bureaucracy. Rather, they are problems of the human heart.*"

"When nations give wars, we should not attend."

"The battlefield of peace is the heart of man."

REVOLUTION

"The good takes time, the bad can be done in a moment. To create a life takes nine months and many years of growth and education; to snuff it out takes a second."

"It is nonsensical to speak of nuclear war. There is only nuclear world destruction."

REVOLUTION

"Just as little as one can learn by being lazy, lose weight by over-eating, stay sober by drinking, be happy by suffering, say the truth by lying, or survive by committing suicide, in a word, achieve an end by doing its opposite —as little can one bring about peace by arming for war."

REVOLUTION

"If only a fraction of the effort used
for preparation and conduct of
war would be used for research into
peace, the chances of man's survival
would be immeasurably increased."

REVOLUTION

"The science of peace is still in the mythical stage. One opinion seems as good as another and everyone believes himself to be an expert. What we need is a science of peace as precise as the sciences of physics and chemistry."

"It is with moral illness that wars begin."

REVOLUTION

"*The evil that arose in the man Hitler was neither recognized nor stopped. His success is due to a universal ignorance of the conditions of peace, a global inertia. We did not possess the consciousness of evil, let alone the will and power to crush it. We had no standards of good and evil, in spite of all our knowledge and philosophy.*"

"Just as peace is indivisible so is Democracy. Only world-wide democracy can guarantee world-wide peace."

WHERE DO WE
GO FROM HERE?

Where do we go from here?

Robert Hartman died in 1973, at the age of 63, with much of his best thinking incomplete, with much of his writing unfinished, unpublished, and as such, unread. It is now up to a new generation of thinkers and doers to carry on the work he began. We need to understand Hartman's thought in all its potentially broad applications. We need to refine it, advance it, and make it known to a broader audience. It is incumbent upon all of us to "build the foundations of the moral society of the future."

"With the practice of axiology begins the new science. The creation of the system is only the structure which enables us to climb up to the high plateau. Before us now stretches the new horizon. Formal axiology, to be a genuine science, must be applicable to the whole vast panorama of the realm of values."

"It took the whole of history so far to unify the world in body and mind. Now we must unify it in spirit."

"This is man's potentiality of becoming. In every man we must see, foster, and educate the possibility of growth. We must abolish all forms of compulsion which obstruct the physical, mental, or spiritual growth of men, whether it be the crippling effect of material poverty, the strait-jacket of totalitarian dogma, or the insanity of prejudice."

"The age of quantity and force is at an end, the age of quality and spiritual power must begin."

REVOLUTION

"The natural sciences have developed methods which have brought gigantic natural powers within the reach of any individual able to turn a switch or push a button. Similarly, ethics will have to develop methods which will bring the moral powers of man within the reach of every individual. There will never be a moral push button, but there may be moral expertness."

"If we understand that to the global science of this age belongs a global power of compassion, that the power of technology today has to be matched by the power of religious consciousness — then we have grasped the secret of this time and age."

"We have found that learning these laws changes the character of the young people, makes them more aware, more awake, and more sensitive."

*"Just as today mathematics is
the language of natural science,
axiology will then be the language
of value science."*

REVOLUTION

"As the men of the Renaissance
began the building of the natural
sciences on which our technological
society is founded so the pioneers
of ethical science must build the
foundations of the moral society
of the future."

"We are at the rudimentary beginnings. With the practice of axiology begins the new science of valuation."

REFERENCES

This is a key to understanding the shortened references provided with each quote in the quote book, along with citation of each according to APA format.

LECTURES refers to Five Lectures on Formal Axiology.
Hartman, R.S., 2019. *Five lectures on formal axiology.* (C.G. Hurst, Ed.). Salt Lake City: Izzard Ink Publishing.

STRUCTURE refers to The Structure of Value.
Hartman, R.S. (1967). *The structure of value.* Carbondale: Southern Illinois University Press.

REVOLUTION refers to The Revolution Against War.
Hartman, R.S. (2020). *The revolution against war.* (G.G. Hurst, Ed.). Salt Lake City: Izzard Ink.

KNOWLEDGE refers to The Knowledge of Good: A Critique of Axiological Reason.
Hartman, R.S. (2002). *The knowledge of good: Critique of axiological reason.* (A.R. Ellis & R.B. Edwards, Eds.). New York, NY: Rodopi.

FORMS refers to Forms of Value and Valuation: Theory and Application.

Edwards, R.B. & Davis, J.W. (Eds.)(1991). *Forms of value and valuation: Theory and applications.* Lanham, MD: University Press of America.

> *[Note: two chapters in this edited volume were written by Hartman. Those chapters are the ones quoted in this book.]*

FREEDOM refers to Freedom to Live: The Robert S. Hartman Story.

Hartman, R.S. (1994). *Freedom to live: The Robert S. Hartman story.* (A.R. Ellis, Ed.). Atlanta, GA: Rodopi.

MANUAL refers to The Hartman Value Profile (HVP) Manual of Interpretation.

Hartman, R.S. (2006). *The Hartman value profile (HVP) manual of interpretation (2nd ed.).* Knoxville, TN: Robert S. Hartman Institute.

PARTNERSHIP refers to Partnership of Capital and Labor.

Hartman, R.S. (unpublished manuscript). *Partnership of capital and labor: Theory and practice of a new economic system.* Knoxville, TN: Robert S. Hartman Institute.

For more information on Hartman, his work, his legacy,
and the Institute that published this book,
visit hartmaninstitute.org.